THE HORSE OF THE MOONLIGHT

By

Irene Taafaki

Illustrated by
Jeff Wakeford

GR

GEORGE RONALD
OXFORD

George Ronald, *Publisher*
Oxford
www.grbooks.com

© Irene Taafaki 1981
Illustrations © George Ronald Publisher Ltd 1981
All Rights Reserved

Reprinted 2014

ISBN 978–0–85398–111–4

The Horse of the Moonlight

WHEN you look out of your bedroom window at night what do you see? This is the story of one special night when a boy called Tim gazed at the sky.

It was a frosty winter's night and Tim was lying in his warm bed. He had just finished a very exciting book but now he was tired. He put his book on his pillow by his head and then gazed up out of his bedroom window into the night. There was a clear black sky with no clouds at all. The moon was shining and the sky was full of brilliant stars. Tim tried to count each one . . . but there were so many.

Then Tim saw something that made him stop counting. He looked very hard. Was one star moving? Maybe it was a satellite, an aircraft or could it be a shooting star? Tim closed his eyes, then he opened them and looked again. Yes, something certainly was moving through the sky and was coming closer and closer to his bedroom window.

As it came nearer Tim saw it was a beautiful white horse flying through the black sky. Tim loved horses but this was the most wonderful horse he had ever seen. It was silvery white just like the moonlight, and there were two beautiful white wings outspread at its sides. It was a horse of the moonlight!

The horse flew down and landed in the garden outside Tim's house. Quickly Tim jumped out of his bed and tiptoed quietly out of his bedroom. He ran downstairs and out of the front door. The night air no longer felt cold; only warm and full of the promise of adventure.

There was the horse of the moonlight standing on the grass. Its silvery wings were folded against its sides and its long mane shone brightly. Tim walked quietly towards the wonderful horse and, as he came close, it lifted its head and turned to Tim. It spoke in a silvery voice.

'I have come to take you on a journey, Tim. Climb on my back so that we can leave without delay!'

Tim didn't feel at all frightened. Without asking a question, he climbed onto the horse's back and held on tightly to the silver mane. The horse of the moonlight spread its silver wings and flew up into the night sky. Soon they were flying high over the sleeping world. Below, Tim could see the dark houses and trees and then the shining water of the sea. Ahead Tim could see mountains, their tops white with snow.

The horse spoke again: 'We are going down to the foot of those mountains. Hold on carefully, we will soon be there.'

Down they flew to the gentle slopes at the base of one of the mountains. The horse landed among the trees outside a stable. Tim looked at it curiously. It was a neat wooden building with one door and a window high in the roof.

'Do you like exciting stories Tim?' the horse asked. Tim nodded. 'Good,' the horse continued, 'I have some friends who stay in this stable. Tonight they want to tell you some stories that are wonderful and true. Open the stable door quietly and go inside.' With that the silver horse spread its wings once more, flew up into the starry sky and was gone.

Tim's heart throbbed with excitement. Very quietly, he opened the stable door. Inside it felt warm and he could smell the sweet, fresh hay. The moonlight shone through the high window and Tim could see three quite old, but beautiful horses standing among the bales of golden hay. They were quietly eating and as Tim softly closed the stable door behind him, all three looked up. One stallion, a fine red roan, spoke first:

'Welcome Tim. We have been waiting for you. Sit down here with us and make yourself comfortable.'

Tim sat down, without a word, on one of the bales of hay beside the three horses.

'Now,' said the red roan, 'who shall be the first to tell his story?'

'Please tell your story first,' said the second horse.

'Yes,' added the third, 'tell us about the time you carried the King of Kings.'

The Red Roan's Story

THE Roan turned slowly toward Tim. The boy saw that the horse's bones were stiff with age, but he held his head high and his eyes grew bright as he began his story.

'Ah yes,' he sighed, 'time has passed and you see my bones are stiff now, but in those days I was a strong stallion. Then I could walk for miles, canter and gallop and never feel a moment's tiredness.

'I was born in Baghdad in the land of Iraq. It was a very old city of historic palaces and mosques with high minarets. Princes, priests, courtiers and nobles had once thronged its busy streets. It was no longer in its former glory – time and war had seen to that. But to me it was still a beautiful city – especially in the spring. How well I can remember one spring. It was a more beautiful and more special springtime than any other. The trees were full of scented blossoms and the first roses of spring filled the air with their wonderful fragrances. The streams were full of water from the melting snows of the mountains near the city, and the river of old Baghdad, the mighty Tigris, was full and swift.

'There was no doubt about it, that was a beautiful spring. And I? I was without question the finest horse in the whole city! My coat was red and glossy, for not a day passed without my being well groomed. After my grooming, my master would ride me with pride through the streets of the city and out into the countryside beyond its gates.

'Early one morning of that spring, I was made ready as usual by my groom. I thought I was making my customary outing into the sweet, fresh country air. Imagine my surprise when I learned that I had been given away! It was a great shock! "Why should my master give me away when I am his favourite steed?" I wondered. I became even more bewildered when I was led from my stable by some men wearing the clothes of those who come from the land of Persia. I had seen these men before, so I knew who they were. They were exiles from their own country. Their Leader, Bahá'u'lláh, had been banished forever by His king, the Shah of Persia, because He was a follower of the Báb. Rather than be separated from their wise and loving Leader, these people had left their property behind them and decided to live away from their homes to be close to Him. These followers of the Báb had been living in our city for about ten years and we had all come to admire each of them greatly. In particular, everyone loved and respected Bahá'u'lláh. Bahá'u'lláh helped all people by His generosity and good advice. His small house was always busy with people visiting Him. No one was turned away, whatever his needs.

'As I was led through the quiet streets of Baghdad in the cool

morning air I came to learn that Bahá'u'lláh was to move away from the city. The Government had invited Him to leave Baghdad and go further away from Persia, this time to Constantinople. "So," I asked myself, "am I to go too?" It seemed so! I can't say I was pleased. I had heard from other horses about the hardships of the long journey to Constantinople. The road across the mountains was rough and dangerous. Little food was to be found along the way, especially just after the winter. No! I had no wish to make such a journey!

'My new owner quietly led me from the old city. We crossed the Tigris to a beautiful garden on the other side. When we arrived, we found a large crowd of folk already there. It looked to me as though the whole city had also crossed the river that morning. There they were – men, women, children, from both rich and poor families. There were those who followed the teachings of the Báb and those who did not. Workmen, princes, priests – I could see them all gathered there and from the look on their faces I could tell that they were all feeling the same way. Not a smile could be seen. Many were sobbing loudly and bitterly. Others just stared, silently, with tears streaming from their eyes. How was it possible for their beloved Bahá'u'lláh to be taken away from them like this? Who could they turn to in times of trouble after He had gone?

'Bahá'u'lláh, His son who was called 'Abdu'l-Bahá, and others of His companions had been in the Garden for twelve days. Afterwards I heard that they had been very special and wonderful days because, in that lovely garden outside my city, Bahá'u'lláh had told His companions that He was the One Promised by the Báb. It was Bahá'u'lláh who was the great Teacher sent by God to guide and unite all the people of the world. This truth was seen by the companions of Bahá'u'lláh as clearly as they could see the sun at the noon of a fine day! Of course many of them had guessed this already because Bahá'u'lláh was so much more wise and loving than any other person they had ever met. All those in the Garden rejoiced and thanked God with all their hearts. All felt very close to God at that time. Bahá'u'lláh called the Garden "Riḍván" which means "Paradise", because it is in Paradise that we are closest to God.

'Every day the friends in the Garden would gather in and

around Bahá'u'lláh's tent. They would sing and pray – praising and thanking God. Their greatest joy was listening to, and reading the words of their Beloved, Bahá'u'lláh. The nightingales sang loudly through each day and night and the air was filled with the perfume of the many beautiful roses cut daily by the gardeners and piled high in Bahá'u'lláh's tent.

'Back in Baghdad the ladies and servants had been very busy packing up Bahá'u'lláh's household. After nine days, they too had crossed the river and joined the happy companions in the Garden of Riḍván.

'I was led into the Garden on the twelfth day. All was ready for Bahá'u'lláh and the Holy Family to leave the Garden with its roses, nightingales, and all the people of Baghdad who loved Him so much.

'As I stood gazing at this scene, I was carefully saddled. When this was done I was led into the presence of Bahá'u'lláh. It was to be my good fortune to be the horse of this Person so loved by all my city. No longer did I fear the long and difficult journey away from my city, for I too was to be in His loving care. You can imagine how honoured I felt when Bahá'u'lláh took my reins in His hands. With great dignity He mounted my back. Then with His son, 'Abdu'l-Bahá, walking beside Him, the One who had become known to all as the Blessed Beauty, began His long journey of exile once again. The rest of Bahá'u'lláh's family and friends followed behind. As we passed through the gates of the garden I heard the call "Allah-u-Akbar" – God is the Most Great – echo over the city from the mosque. As the crowds who were lining our route heard it, they wept more than ever. Many of those standing along the way were pleading with Bahá'u'lláh not to go away from them; did they not know that it was never His wish to leave? He was obeying the Governor. Some of the crowd bowed to the dust at my feet. ME – Sa'údí! His horse! Why! Others even kissed my hooves, many more embraced the stirrups that held His feet. There were some who even threw themselves desperately on the ground before my hooves. They preferred to be trampled to death rather than be separated from their beloved Bahá'u'lláh.

'Carefully, Bahá'u'lláh guided me through these people who loved Him so dearly. He was a fine horseman.

'Many of the people of Baghdad could not bear to lose sight of their Beloved. For several miles they ran along behind Bahá'u'lláh, heedless of the rough and stony road over which we passed.

'After a few miles Bahá'u'lláh gently pulled my reins and bade me stop. He turned and spoke lovingly to those breathless souls who had run so far over such a difficult road. He told them that they should now return to their homes and families in Baghdad and that

they should follow His caravan no further. Bahá'u'lláh reminded the people that he would never forget them and He asked them to show their love for Him by loving and being united with each other.

'How strange it was! Bahá'u'lláh had really been exiled from Baghdad, but right from the beginning His journey across the uplands, through woods, green valleys and pastures, was more like the procession of the King of Kings! There was a guard of soldiers on horseback, fifty mules and seven pairs of howdahs in our long caravan. Day and night, throughout the journey, men sang melodious songs about their love of God and Bahá'u'lláh.

'Those fortunate people who had been able to accompany Bahá'u'lláh worked very hard to show how much they loved Him. Two men walked all the way in front of Bahá'u'lláh – whether He was riding on my back or inside His howdah. These men cooked the food for everyone and washed each utensil afterwards. Only when they were sure that the others were comfortable would they go to sleep. Then they would be the first to be up next day to get breakfast for everyone. All they wanted was that Bahá'u'lláh should be happy, and to serve Him, His family and friends.

'I can remember especially one other man. He took great care of me and also the other horses and mules of the caravan. He wasn't really a groom but a very well-known, rich and wise man who had studied as a Mulla – a Muslim priest. Now all he wished to do was serve Bahá'u'lláh and make Him happy. He wore very simple clothes and would spend all his days looking for straw and food for us animals.

'Day after day we journeyed on joyfully despite the roughness of the roads and the hard climb over hill and mountain. Almost every time we came near a village all the important people and simple folk would rush out to greet Bahá'u'lláh. The villagers would often prepare food in His honour and some places planned great festivities to celebrate His visit. You see, they had heard about the greatness of Bahá'u'lláh and wanted to show Him how much they loved and respected Him.

'It was when we finally reached Sámsún – a port on the shores of the Black Sea – that my humble part in the journey of Bahá'u'lláh ended. From there the Holy Family took a boat to the city of Constantinople. I had spent one hundred and ten days as the steed of the Blessed Beauty. I remember each precious one of them as the day I carried the King of Kings.'

The Wild Stallion

THE flashing eyes of a dark stallion blazed. He began to speak and again the stable became silent as Tim and the other two horses listened to his clear voice.

'I will tell you the story of the greatest man who ever mounted my saddle! This happened in my youthful years, but I can recall the time as if it were only yesterday.

'From as early as I can remember I belonged to the stable of Prince Malik Qásim in Urúmíyyih. What a fine young stallion I was! My coat was dark and glossy, my mane fine and well-brushed and my tail plaited with ribbon. How I enjoyed walking in the Prince's royal processions! Then I would toss my head high in the air, swing my tail proudly and trot along in time to the clash of cymbal and roll of drums. I was a very proud young horse and I made a vow – a promise to myself – that only a truly great man would every ride me! So, I became very dangerous to all riders as I searched for a real master. They called me a difficult horse but I didn't think I was: it was only that I didn't want just *anyone* to ride me!

'Prince Malik Qásim sent an invitation to the most skilful and clever horsemen. He challenged them to try and break me in, yet none of them were good enough for me!

'What fun I had with them! Let me tell you what I did. First I stood quietly and watched their faces as they came towards me. I could easily tell who was afraid: I could see by their faces and trembling hands. Some men were bolder. They would glare as if to dare me to disobey them! After I had had a good look into their faces I allowed the saddle to be put on my back. Then my fun began! As soon as they placed a foot in my stirrups I reared up onto my hind legs, tossed my head and, with a shrill whinny, galloped off. I pranced and turned until the poor horseman could hold on no longer and fell to the ground!

'After some time no one had the courage even to try to mount me. Every challenge to ride me was refused and I was left alone to do as I pleased.

'I spent my days running wild and free over the Prince's lands. If it was hot I rested in the green shade of a cool glade by the stream that trickled across my meadow.

'The days passed, each one the same. Then everything changed one warm morning. Shortly after the golden sun had risen that day my groom came out to the meadow and called to me. As I came close, he threw a halter over my head. Before long I was being led into the town and through its narrow winding streets to the public square.

'I was surprised. Quite a crowd had gathered. All were talking and shouting with great excitement. It was not long before I guessed what was going to happen. Prince Malik Qásim had challenged someone to ride me! The people of the town were arguing as to who would be successful. Amidst the din I could hear them well:

'"This horse will never be ridden!"

'"Let us see what the Siyyid can do!"

'"How can such a man tame a wild horse!"

'My friends, I can tell you that I was annoyed. I didn't want another contest. I didn't like this mob of people. I didn't like to be ridden at all! Snorting angrily, I shied and tried to gallop off, but my groom knew me well and held my halter with a firm grip. There was no escape.

'"Who on earth has Prince Malik Qásim invited to ride me this time?" I thought crossly. "Maybe a general? Another prince? Could it be the King himself." I stamped my impatient hooves on the dusty road. "Let the contest be over, then I can run free again in my meadow."

'Well now! Imagine my astonishment when instead of a great prince or a mighty general, a very different type of person walked quietly towards me. He was a man who was neither tall nor short. He wore a simple cloak and the green turban of a Siyyid, which told me he was descended from the Holy Family of the Prophet Muhammad.

'The man looked into my face with deep, loving eyes. No one had looked at me quite like that before, not even Prince Malik Qásim who cared about me greatly. Then I felt him stroke my head with kind and gentle hands. At his touch all thought of hurting anyone went right out of my mind. I stopped stamping my impatient hoof and became quiet.

'"I'll take this Man anywhere He wishes," I thought. "I have found my real Master at last!"

'Meanwhile my groom was rushing towards the Siyyid, begging Him not to try to ride me: "He has already thrown the bravest and most skilful of horsemen. Please refuse this invitation!"

'To this the Siyyid replied, "Fear not. Commit us to the care of the Almighty."

'I stood, motionless. He placed His foot in my stirrup and mounted my back. Then, at the command of His clear, gentle voice, I moved forward. I held my head high. To carry this Man was a greater honour than being part of Prince Malik Qásim's processions.

'The huge crowd in the town square gasped and became silent. They were astonished to see me so calm and obedient. Then one man exclaimed, "This is truly marvellous! How could this wild horse be so quiet?"

'Another asked in an excited voice, "Do we see a miracle?"

'After this, many of the crowd ran forward and tried to kiss my stirrups. There would have been quite a crush if my groom and some other of Prince Malik Qásim's attendants hadn't been there to make my way clear. Despite all the commotion, I continued to make my way through the crowd. All the noise in the world couldn't have disturbed me. I was too busy – carefully carrying my precious passenger!

'He directed me along the narrow streets of the town to the public bath. Once there, He dismounted and went inside while I waited patiently at the entrance. After He had bathed, He mounted me again and I returned through the streets to the public square. There was a lot of scuffling behind me and I learned later that many of the crowd who had followed us had rushed into the bath to carry away some drops of the water in which He had bathed. They said that only a person with special powers could have ridden me and so believed that this water must be precious!

'Arriving back at the public square, I saw that Prince Malik Qásim himself had come to greet us. I could see by his face that he was as surprised to see me being ridden as everyone else. The

Prince greeted my Siyyid warmly and then took Him away from me back to his own palace.

'As for me? I was led away by my groom. Back I went to my big, empty meadow. Once again my time was my own and I was free to gallop wherever I wished.

'I never saw my special rider again but I often heard His name. Anytime I was taken through the narrow streets of Urúmíyyih the townsfolk would point and cry, "There's the wild horse that was tamed by the Siyyid they called the Báb!" The Báb – yes! That was how I came to know His name. Through all my long life I never forgot it. Nor could I forget His gentle person, and the ride we had together that beautiful warm morning.

The Warrior's Steed

A THIRD HORSE, scarred with the wounds from many fierce battles, moved slowly forward. He limped, but when he spoke his voice was strong and clear. The time had come for him to tell his story. He turned towards the second horse and said:

'I am a warrior's horse too. You can clearly see the scars on my flanks. I had met many brave men in my life, but I never knew courage or skill until I met Mullá Ḥusayn and the followers of the same Báb you speak of, my friend! Without the Báb I should have no story to tell. In the days of my youth His Blessed Name was on the lips of all the people of Persia, so how could we not hear it! In those days there was great excitement all over the land, not just in the cities and towns, but in the farthest villages in the south of the country and in the far mountains of the north where I had my home. I lived in the Holy City of Mashhad, in the stables of my master 'Abdu'l-Alí Khán. Like you, friends, my Master loved and cared for me more than all his other steeds. That was why I was so surprised to learn one day that he had given me away! I had not been sold, but was to be a gift, along with his treasured sword! What amazed me even more was that the sword and I were presented, not to a prince or a brave soldier, but to a Mullá by the name of Ḥusayn.

'This Mullá was said to be leaving on pilgrimage to the Holy places in far-off Karbilá and I was the horse to carry him there. Every one in Mashhad knew Mullá Ḥusayn for his great wisdom, but I still felt annoyed. "To carry a priest is surely not the work of a war-horse such as I," I protested angrily as I was led away from my old home. After all, Mullá Ḥusayn wasn't a soldier. I had heard people say how his hand trembled as he held a pen; so how could he use my master's heavy sword? As we walked through the narrow streets, I wondered, "Why does he need to ride a war-horse? Wouldn't a smaller pony or even a donkey be better for him? Still, why should I, a dumb animal, ask questions. I must obey my master's wish!"

'As we came near to Mullá Ḥusayns house I saw that a great crowd of eager people had gathered outside. What a commotion there was! The streets were full of tearful mothers with their sons, and sisters with their brothers. All were begging that their men be allowed to go with Mullá Ḥusayn on his journey. I began to think that I should not feel quite so sorry about having Mullá Ḥusayn as my new master. Certainly a great adventure must lie ahead of me if so many others were eager to come along with us.

'It was several days later that we set off. Two hundred and two companions, some mounted and some on foot, left Mashhad, with myself carrying Mullá Ḥusayn in front. A camp was made not too far from the gates of the city. There to my amazement, my new master unfurled a flag, a Black Standard. He held it high in the air for all to see. Then Mullá Ḥusayn gave me another surprise. He took off his head-dress and placed a green turban on his head. I knew that a green turban was worn only by those descended from the Prophet Muhammad and that such men were known as siyyids; but Mullá Ḥusayn was not a siyyid. This was unusual behaviour from a man who had spent all his life quietly studying all the laws of his religion; a war-horse, a sword, a battle flag and now a green turban. Whatever would be next! Well, it wasn't long before I found out!

'It was late one evening in the camp. I was quietly cropping some sweet grass when I heard two of his companions talking. One asked, "What path shall we take, my friend?"

"'We take the road to Mázindarán.'

"'Surely not? We planned to ride to Karbilá.' "'This is not to be,' the other quietly replied.

"The Beloved Báb Himself has sent Mullá Ḥusayn the green turban and told him to wear it on his own head. With the Black Standard unfurled before him he should hurry to the forests of Mázindarán. There he is to give help to Quddús."

"'I see,' nodded the first man; "we should indeed give assistance to such a much-loved follower of the Báb."

'That was how I came to learn where we were going and I quickly passed the word around to the other horses in the camp.

'After some days we began our journey, taking the road that led to Mázindarán. It took many days because we stopped at almost every village we came across. At these places Mullá Ḥusayn and his companions would call the villagers to a special meeting and then boldly speak to them. Of course, it was not so easy for me to understand all they said, but I do remember how they spoke of the kind and gentle Báb. They told the people it was a new Day and that the Báb had brought a new message from God which would bring all men together. If they changed their ways they would be able to see the Glory of God.

'Throughout that long journey more men with their horses and ponies joined our group. Some of these horses had wealthy masters who came from very fine houses; others, and there seemed more of these, belonged to more humble folk such as craftsmen, tradesmen, students and poor priests. As I watched these peaceful people gather together for their prayers each day, I kept wondering how there could ever be a battle? I really was very bewildered! If there was to be no battle why had Mullá Ḥusayn raised the Black Standard and why was there such terrific excitement in the air? We all felt it, every man and beast. It was greater excitement than I had felt before going into the mightiest battle.

'After many days on the road we made camp again. This time the camp was beside a clear-running stream and we were glad to be able to rest in such a beautiful spot. There was a mighty tree standing by the stream which gave us good shade from the hot sun. The weather had been glorious, but then one night there was a terrible storm with strong winds. That gale was so fierce that it snapped a huge, thick branch right off this mighty tree and sent it hurling to the ground. We horses were very frightened and restless. How happy we were to see the sun rise the next morning in a calm, clear sky.

'Three days later, we were harnessed and saddled for the last stages of our journey to Mázindarán. As Mullá Ḥusayn prepared to mount me, he gazed at all his companions who were waiting for his signal to depart. Then Mullá Ḥusayn pointed in the direction of Mázindarán. He called in a voice I shall always remember, "This is the way that leads to our Karbilá!"

'Yet another mystery for a poor horse! I knew that the road to Karbilá was the other way, so what did my master mean now? Then I recalled a story I had heard when I was just a young stallion. A very long time ago, terrible battles had been fought at Karbilá and

the pure Imam Ḥusayn, the grandson of the Prophet Muhammad had been cruelly killed by his enemies on Karbilá's battlefields.

'As I stood musing over these stories of the past, I could hear Mullá Ḥusayn telling his companions that their great trials were ahead of them. I wondered if these trials would be like the battles of Karbilá? Slowly I was beginning to understand this mysterious journey to the forest of Mázindarán. Mullá Ḥusayn said that those of his companions who could not face such troubles should now return home. Soon they would meet great difficulties and they would not be able to turn back.

'I did see some horses turned around by their owners. Quietly about twenty of them took the dusty road back the way we had come. The rest got ready to follow right along behind me, the proud steed of Mullá Ḥusayn. To me, my master was no longer just a wise priest but a true general. He was the great leader of a very special, very different army.

'Mullá Ḥusayn said his morning prayers and then spoke again to the remaining companions. His advice was that they should leave all their belongings behind. They wouldn't be needing them any more. Without question every man obeyed. We horses felt our backs to be a lot lighter once all the saddle-bags were emptied! One horse in particular, who usually walked close to me, was much relieved. He had been bearing a huge satchel of precious turquoise stone that had come from the mine of his master. Now that satchel was thrown, along with all the rest, onto the side of the road, just as if it were a bag of worthless sand.

'Once this was done the party set off. The sound of the joyful songs filled the morning air. Yet these were not the fighting songs of war, but hymns of praise to God and the Lord of the New Age.

'We had not long to wait before our first encounter. It happened just outside the town of Bárfurúsh. There was an important religious leader in that town who hadn't even tried to understand the Báb's teachings. He really hated the Báb's enthusiastic and well-behaved followers and wanted to harm them. By doing this he hoped other people would be afraid to listen to the New Message. When this religious leader heard that we were riding towards Bárfurúsh, he encouraged the townsfolk to get any weapon they could find and attack Mullá Ḥusayn and his companions. As he was such an important leader, many of them obeyed.

'As we came to a quiet leafy glade they appeared quite suddenly from behind the trees. I could see their eyes were fierce and their faces full of anger. They shouted abuse at the Bábis, who in return said nothing, but remained silent and very still. Then, the townsfolk began their attack. At first Mullá Ḥusayn refused to allow his companions to fight back. It was not until the seventh of our number fell from his horse that he prepared to defend the lives of his much-loved friends.

'What happened next is impossible for me to forget. Mullá Ḥusayn took his sword from its sheath. Digging his heels into my brown flanks, he spurred me on. Right into the middle of the attackers we went as Mullá Ḥusayn pursued the man who had killed his seventh companion. He feared neither the angry faces nor the weapons that surrounded him. The wretched man we were chasing tried to hide behind a tree. He was trembling and could not face Mullá Ḥusayn, so he held his musket in front of him as a shield. Faster, faster still I galloped. As we rushed towards the tree my master raised his sword and delivered one terrific stroke. My friends! That one stroke cut right across the trunk of the tree, shattered the barrel of the musket and severed the body of that wretched man. One stroke! I could hardly believe my eyes, yet as I have told you, I was Mullá Ḥusayn's charger and so was the closest to that brilliant act. Everyone was stunned. The grove which had rung with the shouts and shots of the ambush grew silent with awe. After many seconds of stunned silence our ambushers fled in panic from the scene. The anger on their faces had changed into fear and amazement at the sight they had witnessed. Our first encounter had ended.

'I was a war-horse and no stranger to fierce battles, but in all my life I had never seen such heroic deeds as those of Mullá Ḥusayn. That day was the first of the many occasions in which we were all able to witness his courage, his strength and his great skill. Through his brave example, the meekest of his companions became lion-hearted; he inspired each man and beast amongst us.'

The eyes of the stallion became misty and his tongue silent.

'Please tell us more,' begged the others, their eyes wide with wonderment.

'There is much more for me to tell, my friends.

'Those months in the forests of Mázindarán were filled with many heroic days. I can recount wonderful deeds of courage by many. I can also tell you about the bitter acts of treachery and of the cruelty of those who opposed and attacked Quddús, Mullá Ḥusayn and the other Bábis. I can tell the story of that bitter winter and the hardships of life under siege in the fort of Shaykh Tabarsí when there was a shortage of food and water. Finally, I can tell you the sad story of the day I stumbled when my foot caught in a tent rope. This led to the death of my beloved master – and to my own slaughter. However, let me rest awhile. The night is almost over.'

The stallion closed his eyes and whispered softly, 'Another time my friends, another time. The night is almost over.'

The End of the Night

THE barn was silent once more. Tim sat for a long time on the bale of hay thinking about the thrilling stories he had heard. After a while he noticed that the stable was filling with a different light. He looked through the high window. The stars were fading in the night sky and a bright red sun was rising over the mountains. Dawn had come, bringing a new day. Tim turned to the three horses, but they, like the stars, were also fading from his eyes.

'Please tell me more stories,' he called. 'Don't go away. Red Roan, tell me again about the time you carried the King of Kings!' But the three horses had disappeared. Tim closed his eyes.

When he opened them again, he found himself in his own bed with the sunlight streaming through the window. His mother was standing over him. She was smiling and in her hand was Tim's book that had fallen from his pillow during the night.

'You must have been having a lovely dream, Tim,' she said.

'I was,' Tim replied. 'A horse of the moonlight flew me far from here to a stable among some mountains. There I met three

horses and they told me their wonderful stories about the Báb and Bahá'u'lláh.'

'That truly was a special dream,' said Tim's mother. 'Why don't you tell me the stories after our morning prayers?'

And that is exactly what Tim did.